The Unwritten Rules of Life

Volume I

By:

Stepan Stepanian

This book is dedicated to my Grandmother, who raised and taught me about the important rules of life and made me the person I am today.

This book is also dedicated to the loving memory of my cousin, Hagop Minassian, who taught us all the most important rule of life; to appreciate and live it to the fullest, no matter what.

This book is a compilation of the many different rules of life that most of us have heard, but have never really had explained. There will be a few rules in this book that will sound very familiar to a lot of people, but there will also be those few rules that many people have never heard of. These are rules that go without say; most of the time people follow these rules without even knowing that such a rule exists. Many of the rules are part of the unwritten rules of "man code", while the majority of them concern both men and women. If you use this book as a guideline in your everyday life, you will notice that things will become much clearer and easier to deal with.

The Rules

The Golden Rule

Although this is one rule that is written in the Bible, it is still one of the oldest and most important rules in life. The rule simply is: to do to others what you would have them do to you. In other words, if you treat others with disrespect, hate, anger, envy, jealousy and any other negative emotion or act, you should expect to receive the same type of response from them toward you. If you treat others with respect, courtesy, love, reverence and any other positive sentiment, you can expect to receive the same reaction from them. Do not treat others like they are worthless and act surprised if they return the same attitude towards you.

Man Up

This rule can be summed up in one very easy sentence: simply, take responsibility for your actions. If you decide to do something, make sure you are prepared for the consequences of your actions. It is very easy to do something and then sit back and point fingers at others, blaming them for the things that you have done, especially when things do not go the way you planned. Life is full of mistakes and bad decisions, be an adult and own up to yours. Even if the outcome is very bad, at least you can walk with your head held high by taking responsibility.

Life Is What You Make It

T he title of this rule can pretty much speak for itself. Whether you are a millionaire, vacationing in all of the hot spots around the world, or a parent of two working a 9 to 5 job trying to make ends meet, your life is what you choose it to be. The bottom line is whether *you* are happy with the life you are leading. Those people who always want more than they have will often find themselves doing just that for the rest of their lives: wanting. However, those who are happy with what they have and appreciate the life they are leading, they make their lives that much better. It's all relative to you and your attitude towards life.

Be Careful What You Wish For...

This is almost a continuation of the previous rule. Basically put, be careful about the things you think you want and focus more on the things you know you need. It is very common to want more things, a faster car, a bigger house etc. However, having all these things do not necessarily equal happiness. Just because something makes someone else happy, it does not guarantee your happiness, too. This does not mean you should not want things you do not have, but it in fact means you should make sure you want those things for the right reason.

It's Just A
Glass Of Water

We have all heard the sayings; the glass is half full versus the glass is half empty. These statements correspond to optimists and pessimists, respectively. This rule, however, is the realists' approach. In other words, it does not really matter the amount of water that is in the glass, all that matters is you recognize that there is water in it. A real world example of this would be a pessimist complaining that a task is too difficult versus an optimist who finds the task very simple versus a realist who just performs the task because it needs to be done.

Keep Your Eyes On The Prize

When you set a goal for yourself, whether it is something as simple as waking up at a particular time to get some extra work done in the morning or something a little more complex, such as starting a small business, set a goal for yourself and follow through with it. Dreams can only come true if you make them a realization in your life. You have to drive yourself and believe in yourself that you will be able to reach your goal, and if you keep a clear image in front of you, physically or mentally, achieving that goal will become easier. If you continue to focus on the outcome you want, you will eventually reach it.

Yesterday is History
Tomorrow is a Mystery

This is another saying that everyone has heard in one context or another. The rule is simple; do not dwell in the past, move passed it and look on to the future. If you make a mistake, or if a particular event happens which does not work out the way you had hoped, do not remain in the past thinking about the "what if's", or the "coulda, woulda, shoulda's". Instead, learn from those events and look ahead, to the future and set yourself up for success going forward. That is not to say do not think about the past at all, just do not let it consume your every thought and allow the present and future to just go by ignored.

It Ain't Over 'Till The Fat Lady Sings

Whether in sports, at work, or even in your own personal life, this has been an unwritten, yet often spoken, rule of life. The bottom line here is; do not give up too soon, because you never know what is waiting for you around the corner. At times it may seem like the only thing left to do is throw in the towel. If you observe anyone, especially athletes, when the going got tough, they got tougher and they did not give up until the last second of play. Sure, it is far easier to call it quits when a few things do not go your way, but you have to push yourself passed the adversities and tough it out all the way to the end.

Hi, My Name Is...

In a world filled with over 6 billion inhabitants, there are many different types of people from many different walks of life. The rule here is to simply be yourself and not try to be someone you are not just to impress others. Sometimes, it is easy to forget who you are or what makes you unique from the rest of the world, especially earlier in life and in school. You have to remember, though, it is that uniqueness that makes you who you are. Do not be afraid to be yourself. There will be plenty of people who will not like you in life, and you will want to change yourself to gain their approval, but those who respect you for who you really are, are the only people you need to worry about.

Don't Hate the Player…

Jealousy and envy are two of the most common emotions that people feel. We all want what we do not have and the more people we see that have it, the more we want it. It is normal to feel this way, but it does not mean there should be hatred or anger towards the people who have what you want. Just because someone has a better car or house than you, or dresses in more expensive clothes than you, or even is better at doing things than you, it does not give you the right to hate on them. Instead, you should use that energy to better yourself and turn the tables on them so instead of being a hater, you will be the one that people want to emulate.

Lead...Follow... Get Out of the Way

Sometimes in life, people find themselves going with the flow of their surroundings. It is easier to walk a path that has already been laid out in front of you rather than trying to create your own. While the majority of the time this could be a good thing, you have to find it in yourself to create your own path and not always follow others. Try not to get caught up in the current of those around you and accept it as the only way. You have to create your own path and be a leader, and not always just a follower.

Actions Speak Louder Than Words

We have all heard this saying at one point or another in our lives. This is perhaps one of the most universal unwritten rules of them all, as it pertains to many different facets of life. It is very easy to say things, such as 'I love you' or 'You're my best friend', but if your actions do not match what you are saying, then your words hold no value. Do not take on extra tasks at work, or try to comfort friends or family by saying things you do not intend to show or do. Just saying the words are not enough, you have to follow through with what you are saying with the things that you do. Do not say things you do not mean, as this will only lead to confusion or people getting hurt.

"I Think I Can"
"I Don't Think I Can"
You're Right

Having faith in yourself is perhaps one of the best motivators you will ever need to succeed in life. If you look at a situation or an obstacle and believe that you can make it happen, then before you know it, it will become a reality. At the same time, if you look at a situation and think to yourself that there's no way you could ever accomplish it, then you might as well not even try because you have already doomed yourself to failure. If you have the right mindset and the belief that you are the owner of your own destiny, then there is absolutely nothing you can not achieve. Stay positive, have faith in yourself, and you will see that all your hopes will become real.

Fear Knocked On The Door, Faith Answered, There Was No One There

There is nothing to fear but fear itself. If you have never heard this saying before, pay close attention. Fear is perhaps the most common and easiest form of release from responsibility. At the same time, it is the most powerful negative emotion people can have. Do not give in to fear, but instead accept that there are some things that will frighten you, but that fear will only drive you further to getting to where you want to go. If you allow fear to overcome your mind, there will be no room left for its adversary, hope. Stand up to your fears face to face and do not allow them to take control of who you are or who you have the potential of becoming.

School Does Not Prepare You For This

There are a lot of differences between book smarts and street smarts. Just because a person is an honor role student, or gets the highest marks in all of their classes, it does not necessarily mean they are smarter than a person who is an average student. School does not necessarily prepare you for the real world; it only prepares you for higher levels of education. The only way to learn the real responsibilities of life is to experience them for your self. There is no way to learn how to deal with the trials and tribulations that the real world throws at you from simply reading a book. There are some things that you have to experience on your own to fully understand them.

Go Team, Go Team Go

From the time we are young children to well in to adulthood, we become fans of sport teams, and also their athletes. We begin to wear the teams' colors, jerseys, hats and other sports paraphernalia. We become loyal fans and stick with the teams through thick and thin. There are those, however, who decide to continuously change the team they are rooting for because their team is performing poorly or because their friends are for the other team. Do not become a bandwagon. If you truly are a fan of a team, stay a loyal fan, whether they are winning the championship or they have the worst record. Do not keep changing your mind because you want to root for the more popular team.

The Number Does Not Matter

At some point or another, we've all heard the saying, "It's not about quantity, it's about quality". This is true in all areas of life. It does not matter how many friends you have, or how many people you know, or how many relationships you've been in. What matters is the quality of those relationships and those friendships. You can have hundreds of friends but if you do not have a best friend, someone you can count on and trust, then the number really doesn't matter. You could have been in many relationships but if you never really loved someone, then those relationships do not really matter. It's not about how much you have; it's about what you do with what you have.

When In Rome...

. . .Do as the Romans do. In other words, know where you are and act appropriately in that environment. This rule is easy enough to understand, however there are countless times when people are in a certain location and act as if they are somewhere else. For example, when you are at work, you should display professionalism and maturity and not exhibit the same type of demeanor as you would at home or around your friends. Know your surroundings and audience, other wise you will inevitably do or say something that others will find inappropriate or offensive, which may lead to unneeded hostility and maybe even termination from your job.

Everything I Say Is a Lie...Except That

The easiest way to explain this rule is simply, do not lie. There are many situations where a lie would appear to be the better route to take rather then telling the truth, for example, when you're trying to spare someone's feelings, or when you are telling a little white lie. The reality of it, though, is the truth would hurt a lot less in the long run. Most of the time with every lie, you will have to think of at least two more lies to cover up the initial one. This number will exponentially grow, and it will come to a point where you have to remember all of the lies to keep your story strait. All of this can be avoided by simply telling the truth from the beginning.

Oh Yeah? You Want To Hear Something Better?

The most irritating thing that a person can do is try to one-up a story that someone else is telling. These people like to wait until someone is done talking to tell a story that is better or more exciting than the one that was just told. This can become very annoying, especially when that person is not part of the conversation. Most of the time, the stories do not involve the person, but a friend of theirs, or their real story is boring so they compensate by adding things to it that did not truly happen. If you are one of these people, do not try to drill yourself in to a conversation and then try to one up every one else to try and show how much better you are, because chances are, you're not.

Think Before
You Speak

Often there are those who say things without fully thinking through them. While this can work some of the time, more often than not, realizing what you are about to say before you say it can save you from a lot of misunderstanding and frustration. Do not just blurt out the first thing that comes to mind before fully understanding the situation first. Just because you are thinking something, and you believe that what you are thinking is correct or even funny, realize who your audience is and try to imagine what their reaction would be before you let the words out.

Oh, You've Seen It? Then Shut Up!

Everyone has experienced this at some time or another. You are getting ready to watch a movie or a TV show, or even a sports game which you have pre recorded and someone just blurts out the ending. While sometimes this happens by accident and the person giving away the ending does not realize that they did anything wrong, often times it is done intentionally. For all those who just want to ruin the outcome of movies and events for others, before you do, ask yourself how you would feel if someone continuously did the same to you. Then you will realize how annoying and irritating it is.

C'mon Now, Be Nice

Y ou can catch more flies with honey than with vinegar. This saying has been around for years and it still holds water, even today. The basic concept behind it is the nicer you are the more you will get out of life. In other words, common courtesy is the ultimate universal language. It does not matter where you are or who you are with, being courteous will always be more beneficial than being rude. Open doors for people and allow others to give their opinion. Even if you know they are wrong, do not interrupt someone when they are talking. Start being considerate to others and you will see that same courtesy given back to you.

Hey, Say Something...

Do not be afraid to speak your mind, when it is appropriate, of course. Sometimes people have great ideas or can add a lot to a conversation that others are having, but they are afraid to speak up because they may be ridiculed or laughed at. Do not hide behind that fear. If you believe that what you are going to say is fitting and suitable for the conversation, do not be frightened to say what is on your mind. If you do, you will inevitably say to yourself later on, "I wish I had said…"

Duhhhh

Common sense is something everyone has but not something everyone always use. People come across many different situations throughout their day in which they use common sense to figure things out. However, there are those who do not seem to have the ability to use common sense in certain situations. There are many examples of common sense situations, and even as you are reading this rule, you have probably already thought of many of them. That little voice of common sense you hear while you are trying to decide whether or not to peruse something, listen to it; it will be the best friend you have ever had.

The Book Was Much Better Than The Movie

In essence, this rules basic meaning is not to be condescending to others. Unfortunately, the need for some people to show how much better they are at something than others is monumental. Far too often, people try to show they are special, and because you have not experienced what they have, a regular person like you could not even imagine how wonderful their life is. Do not talk to someone as if you are more important then they are. Engage in the conversation as equals and you will find that there may be some things that even you did not know and both parties will gain from the exchange.

Know Your
<bank> Roll

In this country, and all around the world, the amount of debt people accumulate grows exponentially every year. This is caused mostly because people spend a lot more than their income. While some of this debt is for important things, such as a college education, housing or food, more often it is driven by jealousy and greed. Do not spend beyond your means. If you can only afford to get the less fancy car or the smaller house, or the non name brand whatever, then that is what you should buy. Of course, the luxury items will make you feel good because you will have something others do not have, but you are the one that is going to be left with the bill, not them.

Money Ain't A Thang

We have all heard the saying, "money isn't everything" or at least some variation to it. What people need to stop doing is worshipping money. It is true; money is not everything in life. Sure, money will definitely alleviate a lot of headaches for people and it would make life that much easier, however it is not a necessity to have all the money in the world. There are plenty of people, some which you may know, or you may even be one of these people, who are happy with what they have and make the most out of the money they are currently earning without so much as a single complaint. It is a harder road to travel, but it is not an impossible one.

Stop Being Greedy

The greed of many big companies and banks is one of the main reasons of the deterioration of the US economy, as well as the world economy, over the last couple of years. On a more personal level, greed often causes trouble and heartache to relationships and individuals every single day. To want something you do not have is not a bad thing, but to let that desire reach excessive levels in which the more you get the more you want will ultimately lead you down a path of greed that no amount of possessions will satisfy and you will always want more.

If The Shoe Don't Fit Don't Wear It

There are a lot of people out there that wear clothes that do not fit them properly. Either the clothes are too big or way too tight. If you have to walk with your legs spread wide in order to prevent your pants or shorts from falling off, perhaps its time to invest in a smaller waist size or a belt. And the same goes for the other end of the spectrum. If you are plus size, putting on a top that is medium is not something that is recommended. You should be proud of who you are, no matter what your size is, but there are limitations to that. Nobody wants to see your underwear through your sagging pants, and nobody wants to see your 'ass-belly' hanging out of the extra small tube top or t-shirt.

Yeah I Have One...
At Home

Everyone has been in a situation where they ask those around them for something and the response they get does not help in the situation at all. For example, you are with a group of people and you ask if anyone has a piece of gum. Someone inevitably will say that they have a piece but it is in their car, which is a mile away. Once again, this response does not help in this situation. If someone asks you for something they need at that moment, and you do not have it in your possession, it is better to say you do not have it rather than giving an anecdote about yourself.

You Smell That?

So here is the deal, you have to realize that you are not the only person in this world and that you are part of a society that has certain standards. One of these standards is basic hygiene. You have to clean yourself up, including your body and your clothes. There is always that one person in the group who believes they do not need to use deodorant or that chooses not to shower regularly or do laundry when necessary. These people are nose-deaf. They do not realize that they are emitting a foul odor or dirty appearance to others, mainly because no one has ever told them the truth. Well, here it is… clean yourself up before heading out of your house.

My Hat
Goes Off To You

Hats were invented to keep your head warm in the winter, block the sun from your eyes and protection against the elements. However, for some reason, people often wear their hats indoors. There really is no reason to wear a hat indoors, other than being at a sporting event, wearing the teams' hat or color that you are rooting for. You are not protecting yourself from any elements when you are in a house or building; there is no sunlight or cold weather. If it happens to be very cold where you are, either turn up the thermostat or kindly ask the owner of the establishment to do it for you.

Warning:
Drivers In Mirror Are
Dumber Than They Appear

Accidents are often caused, not by those who are driving too fast, but more often by those who think they are the only ones on the road. They believe by driving slowly, they are being safe and responsible. The problem is they do this while driving in the fast lane instead of in the travel lane. Other drivers travel slowly because they are not sure where they are going and are trying to read street signs while moving. If you want to drive slow to be safe, move over from the fast lanes and allow other drivers to pass you. If you are not sure where you are going, pull to the side of the road and allow others to get around you. You do not own the roads or highways, be mindful of your surroundings.

Chivalry Is Not Dead…
It's Just Resting

There are those who would say that chivalry is dead; that men are no longer gentlemen. However, it is not dead as there are many out there that still follow these customs. These gentlemen are unfortunately few and far between. Do not be rude and arrogant; be respectful to those who deserve to be respected. While this rule does allude to the golden rule, it is more geared towards men being chivalrous and classy; opening doors for women, being gracious and considerate. It is not difficult; simply being courteous can go a long way.

Urinal Etiquette

This is one of those rules that apply only to men. For some reason, many guys do not know or understand the rules of using a public restroom. If you are one of these men please read the following carefully. If there are more than two urinals in the bathroom, one urinal should be skipped to allow a buffer zone between yourself and the other person. While using the urinal, look forward at all times and do not let your eyes wander around looking at anything other than the wall in front of you. Do not carry on conversations with another guy who is using a urinal. And most importantly, do not attempt to shake their hand or touch them in any way whatsoever.

Someone Light A Match In Here

This is another rule which applies to using the bathroom, especially a public restroom. It is simply known as the courtesy flush. It is a natural bodily function to have to use the bathroom but for the sake of those who are in there with you or those who will be using the bathroom after you, give an extra flush of the toilet near the beginning of your toilet sitting process. This will alleviate the odor from lingering and everyone in the general vicinity will greatly appreciate it.

Blood Is Thicker Than Water

Family always comes first, not matter what. It does not matter where you are or what type of situation you have gotten yourself into, your family will always be there to support you in everything you do. Family, however, does not just mean your blood relations, but it also includes those close friends you may have acquired through the years that you can truly count on. In this regard, the rule here is to always show respect and appreciation to your family over anyone else. Do not sell out your family; because they are the only ones that you can truly trust and count on to be there for you, while those whom are pretending to be your friends will sell you out the first chance they get.

Mistakes Are
Lessons In Disguise

Everybody makes mistakes, nobody is perfect. This is a fact of life that every one should be aware of. If you believe you are someone that never makes a mistake, then you have a belief that is not based in reality. It happens to the best of the best and the worst of the worst. What determines the type of person you are is what you do next. Every mistake has the potential to help you grow as a person and help you to gain experiences that will come in handy later in life. This is only possible, however, if you actually learn from your mistakes and do not allow those mistakes to become habits.

Is It Bright In Here, Or Is It Just YOU?

Here is yet another fashion faux pas that more and more people, especially the younger generation, exhibit. Wearing sunglasses indoors is perhaps one of the latest fashion trends that are both unnecessary and un-cool. Most of the time, people where their sunglasses in clubs or areas that are so dark that it is hard to see, even without any thing covering your eyes. If your eyes are sensitive to dim light, perhaps you should make an appointment with your optometrist to have your eyes checked. You may think it is a fashion statement, but the only statement you are making is you do not realize what time of day it is and you are too stupid to realize that there is no sunlight inside.

Bro's Before Hoes

A classic saying that has been around longer than any one can remember. It is not a hard concept to grasp, but there are areas between the lines that most people tend to ignore. In its simplest terms, this rule states that guys need to stick together as well as girls need to stick together. But there is more to this rule than just the cohesiveness of friendships of the same sex. This is a rule based on the concept of not screwing over, or selling out, your friends to gain brownie points, or favor, with someone from the opposite sex. Stick up for your friends because when the time comes they will stick up for you as well.

Don't Mix *Friendship* With Pleasure

This is another rule which is more or less part of man code, regarding men more than women. The rule states that you should not date or pursue a relationship with a best friend's sister, ex girlfriend or a girl that he is interested in. The reason this rule pertains more to guys than girls is because most of the time, girls do not understand the reasoning behind this mentality. As a guy, you must understand that dating a best friend's ex or sister has consequences and may lead to hard ship between the two of you. This can be avoided by speaking with your friend first, letting them know of your intentions, before pursuing the relationship. It is a simple sign of respect.

The Bank Is Closed

Under no circumstances should you borrow money from a friend. Regardless of the situation, borrowing any amount of money, especially in large sums, will ultimately lead to trouble. Even if your friend is genuine in the intent of trying to help you out and does not want anything in return, you will always feel as if you owe them something. While this may not seem like a big deal to some, you have to understand that friendships should never have any type of owing involved. If there are any disagreements or arguments that occur later on, the money will always be a topic that will come up. It is not worth it. Only borrow money from family, or a bank.

Take One
For The Team

This rule is more often referred to as the "wing-man rule". While it does say wing-*man* it does not just pertain to guys. There are many instances in which women can play the role of a wing-man as well. In essence, this is the basic idea of helping a friend out when it comes to them trying to talk to, or get the attention of someone they are interested in. For example, coming up with an excuse to allow your friend to have some alone time with their pursuit. Another example is going on a double date or dancing with the friend of the person being pursued to allow your friend to dance with or feel comfortable on the date, even it is not someone you are interested in or attracted to.

Curiosity Killed The Cat

Many people have, what some would consider, a very bad disease in which they need to know what is happening in everyone else's personal lives. Whenever these people are in a public place, their eyes are always wandering around trying to see what every one is up to, trying to read peoples lips to see what they are saying, if it is anything about them. These types of people also live on gossip and go through great lengths to find out all the dirt and what people are doing in and around their community. This is not a good life to lead. Do not be concerned with the business of others' and do not be nosey. If there is something that concerns you, chances are you will find out sooner or later.

Is The Enemy Of My Enemy My Friend Or My Enemy?

Keeping your friends close but your enemies' closer is a concept that has been around for a long time; however the explanation of this rule continues to elude some people. The meaning is simple; your friends are those people you can trust and count on at all times. You do not have to worry about them, for the most part at least, stabbing you in the back or betraying you. Enemies, on the other hand, you cannot trust and therefore you would need to keep a closer eye on them. This rule does not imply that you should hang out with or invite your enemies over, but it is more to imply that your enemies are the ones you should be keeping an eye on, rather than your friends.

Measure Twice, Cut Once

Do not rush through things, think them through and work out all of the different scenarios that could occur before jumping in to it. Understanding what the consequences would be of the task you are trying to complete will make the task that much easier to handle, given that you would have the proper expectations established. Far too often, people have an idea that they believe is golden. Unfortunately, they do not think it through all the way and they overlook key elements that cause road blocks and obstacles to pop up later on when they are following through with their ideas. Think ahead; it will make things a lot easier for you.

Don't Mix Business With Pleasure

Many companies already have in place rules which frown upon and sometimes even restrict co-workers from engaging in a personal relationship with one another. Whether or not the company that you work for enforces this type of rule, it would be in your best interest not to get involved with someone from work. The reason for this, in case you do not know, is because it would lead to many awkward situations at the office, not to mention the fact that all of your co-workers, in some form or another, would be mixed up in your relationship. Even if this is something that does not concern you, think long and hard about the underlying consequences before pursuing the relationship.

Don't Quit Your
Day Job

The more you know how to do, the more well rounded you will be in life. Unfortunately, there are those that go one step further, and things begin to get messy. Even though their chosen career path is in one profession, they try to meddle in other professions as well. This is sometimes caused by boredom, or by financial motivation. The problem is people often quit their current job right away in order to pursue their idea. This is a huge mistake, especially if you are trying out this new venture for the first time. Keep working where you are and pursue your dream on the side. This way you will always have your current job to fall back on, in case things do not work out as you had planned.

ID Please

Here is another rule that pertains to men only. This rule has been passed down and around in many different circles, however, many have never even heard of it. This is the age rule; the formula which determines what the age difference between a guy and a girl should be to be socially acceptable. This formula does have one caveat, though, which is that true love does not know age, as long as that age is legal! The formula is as follows: the guys age divided by 2 plus 7. For example, for a 28 year old guy, the minimum age of the girl should be 21 $(28 / 2 = 14 + 7 = 21)$. This formula should be used by those between the ages of 22 and 34.

Special thanks to friends and family for their help and contributions to the making of this book.

* 9 7 8 0 6 1 5 4 0 2 9 4 9 *